W9-BDF-411

# Windows 10:

New 2020 Complete User Guide
to Learn Microsoft Windows 10
with 50 Tips & Tricks.
November Update Included.

ISBN: 9781652206118

# CONTENTS

**Thank you for purchasing this book!**

We always try to give more value then you expect. That's why we've updated the content and you can get it for FREE. You can get the digital version for free because you bought the print version.

The book is under the match program from Amazon. You can find how to do this using next URL: https://www.amazon.com/gp/digital/ep-landing-page

**I hope it will be useful for you**.

# Introduction

In July 2015, a new operating system from Microsoft, Windows 10, was released, which, according to the developers, has absorbed the best of its predecessor systems and freed itself from the most annoying shortcomings.

The Top 10 will be the last in the Windows family of OSs, so a universal transition to it is a matter of time.

Seven reasons to install Windows 10 immediately

> Windows 10 is faster than Windows 8 and 7.

> Dozens of protection mechanisms provide the highest level of security among all Windows operating systems.

> Windows 10 has a single interface for desktops and mobile gadgets, which makes it possible to run the same applications on different devices.

> Data synchronization and access to cloud storage provide a Microsoft account.

> "Ten" has a full-fledged Start menu, which was so lacking for Windows 8 users.

In addition, the "Start" can be configured to work with the mouse and keyboard (Continuum mode, in which the menu occupies a corner of the screen) or touchscreen (full-screen mode).

Windows 10 added a lot of useful options: virtual desktops, a fast and well-protected Edge browser, a free Office suite (available for download from the Windows store), the Cortana smart assistant, an improved Snap function (quick switching between Windows), a new OneGet developer interface and etc. There is no need to update the hardware. System requirements for Windows 10 correspond to the level of Windows 7 and 8.

# Chapter 1: Windows 10 November Update

2019 November Update, the update will include the following innovations:

- Management of third-party voice assistants (not just Cortana) on a locked screen;

- creating events in the calendar in a pop-up Window on the taskbar, without launching the application;

- in the Start menu, the navigation panel will expand when you hover over it with the mouse, providing additional information about each icon;

- A search will appear not only on the local Drive , but also in the OneDrive cloud storage.

- The battery life on devices with "some types of processors" will increase (models are not specified).

The public release of the Windows 10 November 2019 Update, codenamed

Windows 10 19H2, took place on November 12. Microsoft considers Build 18363.418 to be the final build, which contains all the new features. Cumulative update KB4524570 (Build 18363.476) includes the latest fixes.

## How to download Windows 10 November 2019 Update (version 1909)

The latest operating system update, version 1909, is the smallest in size compared to previous updates. If you updated your operating system after May, then updating to the November version will take you very little time. But this is only for those users who are not too lazy to update the operating system on time. If you have configured the automatic update function, the process will go automatically.

## What do I need to prepare and check in the OS for the user before installing the

# Windows 10 November 2019 Update, so that after its deployment there will be no problems when the operating system starts and runs?

1. Update the necessary Drive rs, for example, the latest Drive rs for Intel video devices compatible with the November 2019 Update, are already available on the official websites of PC or laptop manufacturers such as HP, Lenovo, Dell and others. Moreover, it's impossible to download and install these Drive rs from the Intel site just like that - the following error will pop up: "The Drive r being installed is not validated for this computer. Please obtain the appropriate Drive r from the computer manufacturer. "This error is due to the fact that now the aforementioned computer manufacturers have specifically made software adjustments to the settings for Intel graphics Drive r updates to prevent downloading and installation of these Drive rs not from their sites, but from third-party sources . So, even

if a user downloads Drive rs from the official Intel website as a zip file and starts manually installing them manually, this error may occur too.

2. Prepare at least 32 GB of free space on the system Drive , it is also possible that more space is required to store intermediate files during the upgrade process. If there is not enough space on the system disk to install the November update, then installing it will fail. It is recommended that you use the built-in Storage Sense utility, which allows you to automatically clean your hard Drive , including temporary files and the Windows Update cache.

3. After installing the Windows 10 November 2019 Update, you will need to restart your computer, so it's better to make a backup of the system before starting installation and save all critical data on a separate medium in advance.

If a six-month update is available for your computer, we'll see a notification in the update center, saying that an optional update of Windows 10 functions to version 1909 is available. And below, a link to start the update process will be implemented.

After the update files are downloaded and installed, we can restart the computer or plan to restart it at a convenient time.

This time Microsoft delivers us an update with a minimum number of changes, it will be installed into the system quickly, like monthly cumulative updates. This means, of course, that we are updating from the version of Windows 10 1903.

And after the reboot, we will already see the new version of Windows 10 1909.

What if you do not have the opportunity to upgrade to version 1909? I recommend not doing anything. The fact is that Microsoft has undertaken to improve the quality of its services and is going to more accurately implement the delivery of six-month functional updates, preventing them from being on those computer devices that may cause problems. It is known that the November update 2019 is not installed on computers with old Wi-Fi Drive rs on Qualcomm chips and with old Bluetooth Drive rs on Realtek chips. Microsoft recommends updating the Drive rs manually and after waiting for the update center to update to version 1909. The obstacle to the possibility of updating is the presence on the computer of old versions of antiviruses.

## What's new in this update?

We already figured out how to install this, now let's look at what new this version of the operating system gives us.

## 1. Improving Productivity and Energy Efficiency

According to Microsoft, the November 2019 Update brought Windows 10 performance improvements through the optimization of individual system processes, in particular those related to the use of a processor resource. In version 1909, a new rotation policy is implemented, within which priority tasks will be distributed among preferred ones, i.e. more powerful processor cores.

In version 1909, portable devices based on individual processors will conserve battery power more economically.

Microsoft also improved the system handwriting, its delays will now become smaller.

## 2. Support for alternative voice assistants

In current versions of Windows 10, only Cortana can work on the lock screen. Microsoft seems to be giving up on Cortana as a consumer product. In 19H2, Cortana will give way to other voice assistants on the lock screen - users will be able to use alternative assistants, for example Amazon Alexa.

This is a small feature that will work automatically after Amazon implements its support in Alexa. You can talk with your voice assistant and get answers directly on the Windows 10 lock screen.

As Microsoft notes: "This change allows third-party digital assistants to activate voice interaction on top of the lock screen."

## 3. Improvements to system notification settings

Minor improvements to Windows 10 functionality in version 1909 include changes to the system notification settings. In the notification settings in the Settings application, the ability to sort applications that deliver notifications to us has been added.

And when you open the notification settings for each individual application, we can choose one of the types of delivery of notifications - either displaying banners or displaying in the notification center. The option to choose the types of delivery of notifications was earlier, but now the types are accompanied by pictures for a clearer understanding by the user what is at stake.

Well, since Microsoft paid attention to such a trifle, probably the company received a sufficient amount of feedback that these settings are implemented slurred.

## 4. Improvements for the Calendar app

Another of the few functional improvements is for the regular Windows 10 Calendar application. Very sensible, by the way, for those who use it. The ability to create new tasks is integrated directly into the calendar pop-up panel in the system tray, the one that appears when you click on the current time.

A simplified form for creating new tasks is integrated into the system tray: we can enter the name of the task in it, select the calendar, specify the time of the task and the location of an object associated with it. If necessary, we can use the Details button to launch the task we started in the Calendar application and complete it there using all the features of the task creation form.

If you still have no opportunity to upgrade to version 1909 after solving problems in the update center, you can try to update the system using the Update Assistant - Windows 10 Update Assistant. Naturally, we recommend that you first back up the current version of Windows 10. Download Update Assistant you can on the official website of Microsoft. Then, run the utility and follow its instructions.

## 5. Universal Search in Explorer

This feature first appeared in Windows 10 20H1, but will become part of the Windows 10 update (version 1909). This feature should make it easier to find files on your computer. An advanced search feature is available in this update. Now in the drop-down menu when searching you will be offered files that are located in OneDrive  cloud storage, and not just on your personal computer. If you need other results, just press Enter and go to the traditional search results.

## 6. Calls in the application "Your phone"

Rapid steps, friends, the standard Windows 10 application "Your Phone" is developing. Let me remind you that this application connects a computer and a smartphone based on Android (not lower than version 7) using a Microsoft account on the Internet. And it allows us to control the smartphone from a computer. The "Your Phone" application is Microsoft's answer to Apple regarding the implementation of iPhone ID technology on Mac devices using Apple ID. The application "Your Phone" appeared relatively recently, in the version of Windows 10 1803, i.e. with the update for the first half of 2018. But by version 1903, it already allowed on a computer to view photos from a smartphone, receive and send SMS, manage notifications, display a smartphone screen in its Window and manage it. True, the latter function only works for a number of the latest Samsung and OnePlus models, and the computer must be compatible with Bluetooth equipment.

In version 1909, the "Your Phone" application was replenished with the ability to make calls. Open the calls section in the application, select the subscriber from the contact list, or dial the phone number. Press the call button.

Well, we communicate with the subscriber on Skype. The call widget will be visible at the top right of the screen. If necessary, we can expand this widget.

And get access to call options, like on a smartphone.

We can also receive calls through the "Your Phone" application according to exactly the same principle as in Skype. When someone calls us, we can accept the call or drop it.

Communication takes place through a microphone and computer speakers, we are not tied to a smartphone. So tired in the evenings, sitting down at the computer to surf or play when someone calls us, we can not get up for a smartphone if it lies far from us. And we can talk to a person like on Skype. To use the call feature, you must also have a computer with compatible Bluetooth equipment.

## 7. The modified principle of signing the final builds of new versions of Windows 10

Microsoft has changed the principle of signing final assemblies of new versions of Windows 10 that existed in 2017. This is the procedure for approving an assembly as RTM, i.e. Builds ready for release and mass distribution to user devices. Well, I mean formally ready, in fact, any new version of the "Ten" is then added two months after the official release. Prior to this, the approval dates for RTM assemblies were March and September, in fact, why the versions of Windows 10 carry the encoded first two digits in the name - the year of update, the second two - month: 1703, 1709, 1803, 1809, 1903, 1909. And already Updates starting in 2017 in the title indicate the month in which their official release took place (without taking into account the facts of withdrawal of updates due to the need for revision): April 2018 Update, October 2018 Update, May 2019 Update, November 2019 Update.

So from now on, months of signing the final assemblies will be June and December. In December, insiders will receive a run-in update for the first half of next year, in June - respectively, for the second half of this year. Thus, Microsoft extends the time for running-in and identifying problems in RTM assemblies from about two months to five to six. This friends, is very good news: at the time of release, we will not receive new versions of Windows 10 as raw as they were the last two years.

So, now there is active testing of Windows 10 20H1 - updates for the first half of 2020. And already in it, we are supposed to see significant new products of the operating system: the new Microsoft Edge browser based on Chromium, cloud recovery of Windows 10, monitoring the temperature of the video card in the task manager, etc.

8. **The Windows 10 version of 1909 has two other innovations - with a minus sign. Consider them.**

# 1. Problems Starting Windows Sandbox in Home Editions

In version 1903, for the first half of 2019, Windows 10 was replenished with a new system component - the Windows Sandbox sandbox. This is an isolated virtual environment for testing dubious software. But Windows Sandbox is only available in editions of Windows 10, starting with Pro. Therefore, the network began to actively distribute manuals and batch files for the implementation of the sandbox component in the Home edition. So, friends, if you are one of those who resorted to this method of obtaining Windows Sandbox, you should better wait with the system upgrade to version 1909. In it, in the Home edition, the embedded sandbox component will not work in a third-party way.

If something, then here you are, friends, the recipe for blocking functional updates to Windows 10.

## 2. Imposing a Microsoft account on the Home Edition

The second unpleasant news for owners of Home Windows 10 is the active imposition of a Microsoft account. If you, friends, have a computer connected to the Internet, at the stage of creating an account when installing the operating  system, you will not be able to choose to create a local account. You will be asked to either log in with your Microsoft account or create a new account.

But you can only create a Microsoft account. The possibility of creating a local account for users of the Home edition is no more.

Fortunately, it is left for editions, starting with Pro. How then to create a local account, if there is a preference to use it? You need to install Windows with the Internet turned off. Those. it does not need to be connected during the installation of the system. And if the Internet connects automatically through a router and an Ethernet cable, then you just need to remove the cable during the installation of Windows. And stick it after installation. You can also turn off the Internet during the Windows installation phase by calling the command line with the Shift + F12 keys and entering the launch command to display network devices:

*control netconnections*

In the Window of network devices in the context menu, turn off the network card.

And turn it on already in the installed system in the opposite way. With the Internet turned off, the ability to create a local account will appear.

# Chapter 2: Installation Windows 10 on your computer.

In fact, installing Windows 10 is no different from installing Windows 8 or 7, only the design has changed, so if you are already familiar with the installation of previous operating systems, then you can easily install this system on your PC. For those who previously did not know how to reinstall the operating system and all the time contacted the service center, where repeatedly they paid exorbitantly large money for this rather complicated at first glance, but in fact, very easy procedure, I say that from now on you will save very, very big money in your budget.

I must say right away that in the process, I will touch upon the moment of how to write the image to a flash Drive or disk because now even the developer of the operating system has begun to encourage this type of installation on users' computers. Such a flash Drive: with a recorded operating system - we recommend keeping it always at hand, so that if for some problems your computer does not work, then you could always fix this situation without any difficulty. Also, in order not to download updates for the operating system all the time, and, believe me, over time they simply become huge, you can update the operating system available on your media.

Now, how to burn Windows to a flash Drive. You of course, can, write this to a disk, with flash Drive s somehow more modern and faster.

 In my opinion, the installation of an operating system from a CD is currently fading into the background. Yes, this is somehow familiar, but the benefits remain with flash Drive s.

## 1. Burn a Windows image to a USB flash Drive

In order to write an image in * iso format to a USB flash Drive, we need the UltraISO utility, which is quite easy to find on the Internet.

1. Launch UltraISO and select "Open" from the "File" menu

2. In the Window that opens, select the Windows 10 distribution image that you downloaded.

3. Now in the "Self-loading" menu, click on the option "Burn hard disk image"

30

4. In the Window that opens, in the "Disk Drive" field, select your USB flash Drive and click write.

5. The program will warn about the deletion of all data from the USB flash Drive, agree and wait until the recording ends.

## 2. BIOS setup

Starting to install the system, we need to go into the BIOS and put in the first place boot from the flash Drive. Turn on the computer or restart it if it is already on. To enter the BIOS, we immediately begin to press the DELETE or F2 key (depending on the motherboard). I need a few seconds until you see the BIOS itself.

1. We can navigate using the arrows and the Enter button on the keyboard.

2. Go to the BOOT tab and find the Hard Drive s item there. We open it.

3. We get to the first point and press Enter.

4. In the Window that opens, he selects his flash Drive and now it will be in the first place. Excellent!

5. ESC to return to the previous Window. Now select the first item Priority boot device.

6. We get to the first point and click

7. Now she selects the download in the first place.

8. Excellent! Now the computer will boot from the USB flash Drive . To save the changes made, press the F10 key and press Enter.

9. The computer restarts ...

It is worth saying that in some BIOSes the interface is slightly different. In this case, you will have to look for similar buttons.

# 3. System installation

1. Installing Windows 10 begins with the language selection Window. Choose your language and click "Next"

2. In the next Window, put one single daw, thereby confirming the acceptance of license conditions

3. Next, in the Window for selecting the type of installation, select "Custom", because we are not updated, but install the OS from scratch

4. In the Window that appears, select the hard Drive  and the partition on which we will install the system

5. After this, the installation process starts, which lasts about ten minutes, wait until the end and automatic reboot

6. At the time of the reboot, we again go into the BIOS as described above and change the boot priority. Now put the

hard Drive first, on which we install Windows and again press "F10"

## 4. System preconfiguration

1. After rebooting, select "Settings" to configure basic system parameters

2. In the new Window, select "Use Express Settings" if you do not want to change the default settings, or "Custom" if you want to change the basic settings.

3. By clicking on the "Custom" item, we can change the settings for automatically updating applications and Drive rs, as well as the privacy settings on the Internet.

4. In the next Window, select whether to allow Windows applications to track our location, as well as use our personal data in third-party applications.

5. After setting up the system, create an account in Microsoft by clicking "Create a new account"

6. In the Window that appears, enter the first name, last name and create a mailbox on one of the Microsoft mail services

7. Next, enter the backup mail account for recovery, or the mobile number

8. In the next Window, enter the captcha and remove the daws about receiving notifications of updates from Microsoft

9. Next, we are offered to verify the account at our request, we refuse by clicking "I can`t do this right now" in the lower left

10. The next Window notifies us that data such as our photos, documents and settings will be backed up to Microsoft Cloud Storage. You can opt-out by clicking "Turn off these OncDrive settings"

11. Next, click "Next" and the installation is complete

P. S. Installing on a laptop or netbook is no different from installing on a regular PC, except in speed, but it depends on which computer and which laptop– or netbook.

Since there are a huge number of motherboards, video cards, sound cards, etc. Then instead of reading a huge amount of information and looking for your equipment, I offer you the option most suitable for all users: download a special program that automatically it will detect your devices and install all the Drive rs on the computer, and you just have to do a system reboot and continue working.

The program is called Drive rPack Solution and you can find it in the public domain on the Internet. There are two options for the program kit, this is complete - with all Drive rs, for all devices, which takes up a lot of space, and also compact, which detects your devices and then downloads only the Drive rs you need from the Internet.

## 5. Drive rPack Solution

I recommend that you select the option "Install automatically", after which, all Drive rs will be installed in auto mode

Do not forget that for the system to work properly, you need to install DirectX, which can be downloaded on the official website of the operating  system developer by simply entering the name of the component in the search bar. This is a small file, only a few kilobytes in size, that will start the online installation and download of all DirectX library files. Many people think that the DirectX library is needed only for video games and graphics, but this is far from the case: a lot of components are used for audio devices and the sound Drive r of a computer. In general, this library is a kind of Drive r that cannot be skipped and not installed. Just run the file on your computer and follow the instructions of the installer.

When a user connects a new device to a computer, the system itself finds the necessary Drive r and installs it. However, earlier this could have caused problems, because not everyone had the Internet, and even if they had one, it was problematic to find the right Drive r. Now, Windows 10, like its predecessor, has further improved the mechanism for installing new devices, as well as searching, if necessary, for the necessary Drive rs.

Now, if you need to connect some device to the computer, but the Drive r is not located, then you should do the following:

Go to the properties of the "Computer" menu and select "Device Manager", then find "Unknown devices" and open the full list, you will see that you may have more than one device working without Drive rs. Double-click on any of them and a Window will open.

If you go to the "Drive r" tab in this Window, you will see that there is a button "Update", click on it and then you will see the following Window with two points for selection:

Automatic search for updated Drive rs; Search for Drive rs on this computer.

In order for the Drive r to be found on the Internet, you need to have an Internet connection and click on the "Automatically search for updated Drive rs" button, then the search process will start, which will either find the Drive r, if it is missing and install it automatically, or it will display a message that the appropriate Drive r is already installed and no updates required.

# Chapter 3: Windows 10 Hotkeys

More about the keyboard. In addition to individual control buttons, Windows uses special button combinations - "hotkeys". It would be nice for us to learn several such combinations from the very beginning.

F + L - opens the Start menu.

E + N - allows you to switch between running programs. To switch to other applications, the N key is pressed several times while holding E. If you also hold Shift, switching in the task list will be performed in the opposite direction.

E + n - closes the current Window.

t - activates the menu bar.

Shift + V - Deletes an object without placing it in the Trash.

Windows 10 also has some useful combinations with the <Win> button located in the lower-left corner of the keyboard. They should be remembered if only because the context menu for the right mouse button is actually not here.

The <Win> key (instead of the Start

menu, as before, opens the start screen of the tiled interface with the icons of installed applications.

Win + Pause / Break - opens the computer properties Window (the same when double-clicking on the Computer icon, holding down the E key);

Win + D - open the desktop and still minimizes and maximizes all currently open Windows.

Win + G - Launches a game console with the ability to record video from the screen.

Win + B - switching between the "tiled interface" and the desktop mode.

Win + E - launch Explorer.

Win + I - Options menu.

Win + Pause - System Properties menu.

Win + X - opens a special shortcut menu to the most useful Windows tools -

Control Panel, Explorer, Computer menu, Command Prompt, etc. Perhaps this is the key combination you will need to memorize in the first place.

Win + R - opens the Run program Window.

Win +. (dot) - pins the current application on the right side of the screen. Use this combination twice, and the application will be on the left side.

Win + M - minimizes all open Windows.

Win + a / c - moves and fixes desktop applications in the appropriate direction or to another monitor.

Win + N - allows you to switch between applications. This combination is similar to using the top-left hot corner.

Win + word set - a quick search for programs by name.

Win + R - take a screenshot and save it as a file in the Images folder.

Win + L - blocks Windows. When locked, the start screen appears on the monitor, and to return to Windows you need to enter the access password again. All running programs at this time continue to work in the background.

Here are a few keyboard shortcuts with the F button:

F + O - open a document (in any program); F + W - close the document (in any program); F + S - save the document (in any program); F + P - print a document (in any program); F + A - select the entire document (in any program);

F + C - copy the selected part of the document or file to the clipboard;

F + V - paste part of the document or file from the Clipboard.

Of course, there are many more "hotkeys" than those listed on this list; moreover, each program has its own combinations. But it is these teams - at least some of them - that you need to master at the very beginning of the work. Check for yourself how long it takes to fuss with the mouse in the menu to give a command to print the text, and then press F + P. Is not that so faster?

# Chapter 4: Gesture control

Owners of tablets and laptops with a touch screen will not have to communicate with the keyboard and mouse - finger gestures will play the main role in controlling the system.

A tap is simply the touch of an icon or

other screen elements. There is a normal and "long" tap, with a delay. Usually, a short tap simply launches the program, and a long one is similar to the right mouse button: in the tiled mode, it calls up the tile properties, and in the desktop mode, it calls up the Context menu.

"Swipe" - a gesture on the screen, without taking your finger off the touch surface. Horizontal swipe from left to right - switching between running tile interface programs. In addition, in tiled mode, a vertical swipe will help you

Select one or more program tiles.

Vertical "swipe" - From top to bottom - closing the application. Bottom-up - call the Command Bar at the bottom of the screen.

And to close the tile mode application, its Window

You need to drag your finger down to the bottom of the screen.

"Pinch" with two fingers. Scaling the image on the screen.

Three-finger gestures:

• 3 fingers up - View tasks;

• 3 fingers down - Show desktop;

• 3 fingers left or right - go to previous applications;

• 3 fingers left or right - E + N (Task View) appears, and you can select the application or the desired Window (remove

Fingers to choose);

• 3-finger tap - Search.

# Chapter 5: Voice control. Cortana

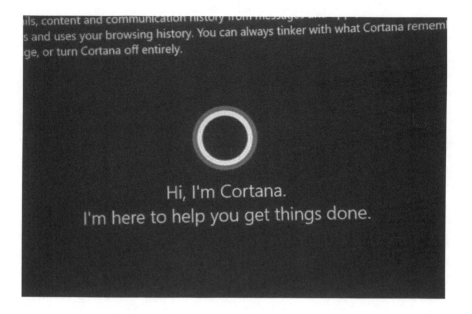

You will not surprise anyone today with voice control and voice assistants: Apple gadget users have been "pardoning" their Siri for six years, and Android with its "OK Google!" Microsoft joined the last voice race - in fact, the debut of its "assistant" by the name of Cortana took place just in Windows 10.

You can use Cortana not only on Windows devices but also on Android gadgets by installing the application on your mobile gadget from Google Play. Together with another wildly convenient function: after installing Cortana, notifications from your Android phone or tablet will also come to your desktop computer or laptop with Windows on board.

.

What can I do with Cortana voice commands?

Launch the program, open a document, create an event on the calendar or call a friend via Skype, set up a virtual alarm clock and even recognize the music from the microphone and give a link to it on the Web ... I'm afraid that I will not be able to dictate a long letter or post on Facebook. But do not forget that we are at the beginning of the road!

The most bonuses from working with Cortana will be, of course, for owners of smartphones and tablets (do not forget that Microsoft's voice assistant can also be installed on Android): Cortana will notify them of new messages, missed calls from a mobile gadget on your computer, and even inform about low battery.

Cortana is available through the search bar at the bottom of the Windows 10 screen in the Taskbar, and you can also call it through the new Microsoft Edge browser and several other built-in applications.

An extended list of voice commands that Cortana understands (available both on mobile devices based on Windows 10, and, partially, on computers and laptops).

Commands for your voice assistant:

1.  Call contact

"Call" contact name " (where contact name is the name of the person in the contact list).

For example: "Call Lisa Miller."

If there is only one phone number in the contact card and you have recently contacted it, a call will be made. If you have multiple phone numbers

the contact will need to select the number you want to dial.

2.  Call to any phone number

"Call" phone number " (where the phone

number is any phone, regardless of whether it is assigned to a contact or not).

3. Redial last number

You should say: "Call back"

4. Send SMS

"Send SMS" contact name "" (where the contact name is the name of the person from the contact list).

For example: "Send SMS to Lisa Miller." This will open an SMS for this user, and then you can dictate the message.

When finished, say "Submit" to send it,

"Add" to add more information to the

message, "Repeat" to dictate the message again, or "Cancel" to cancel the message.

5. Create note

"Note" the text of your note" (where the note text is the text to be included in the note).

For example: "Note to take bread on the way home." The note will be saved and opened in OneNote. Then, you can view and change the text in the note or tap the Sound note item, click the play icon to play it.

6. Opening apps

"Open the application" or "Run the

application" (where the application is any on the phone, for example, "Calendar", "Maps" or "Music" or the applications that you downloaded from the Store).

For example: "Open Calendar"

7. Internet search

"Find" Keyword " or "Search" Keyword " (where the keyword is what you are looking for).

For example: "Find pizza."

Bing will show results depending from what you said, like a map with pizzerias.

Note! If you use Google Chrome as the main browser, don't be too lazy to go into its settings: here, in the Search section, you can enable recognition of the "OK Google" voice command ... And thus, get a second voice assistant - however, its competence extends only to the search field online.

It is funny that Cortana's assistant can be given not only a voice command but also ... a song! You are probably familiar with mobile applications that can recognize almost any melody on the fly, even if you whistle it yourself without being too fake. In this regard, Cortana is still difficult to compare with Shazam or Soundhound ... But in some cases, it recognizes a popular track from a radio or mobile phone. At the same time, offering to buy a song or a full album in the Windows Store.

# Chapter 6: Tips &Tricks

## 1. Windows 10: the most necessary programs and applications

Almost all of these applications are free, so your wallet will not suffer damage. We will download and install them in different ways:

• Most - in the old fashioned way, from the pages of their developers (they are listed next to the name of the application), through a browser.

• A smaller part is from the Windows Store: it is both easier and more practical (programs installed in this way will be updated automatically).

a) Work with archives (compressed folders)

7-Zip - 7-zip.org

b) Cloud Drive s

Dropbox * - Dropbox.com

Google Startup & Sync * (for unlimited uploading of photos to Google's online album) - photos.google.com/apps

 Backbaze (unlimited cloud space for your backups for $ 5 per month) - backblaze.com

c) Backup

AIOMEI Backupper Standart - aiomei.com

d) Create bootable USB sticks from ISO image files

Rufus - rufus.akeo.ie

e) Remote computer control

TeamViewer - teamviewer.com

f) Recover deleted files

Recuva - piriform.com/recuva

g) Malware protection

MalwareBytes - malwarebytes.com

h) Details of your computer

Speccy - piriform.com/speccy

i) Disk Cleanup

Ccleaner - piriform.com

j) Automatic keyboard layout correction

Punto Switcher - punto.ru

k) Application for viewing Internet pages (browser)

Google Chrome - my-chrome.ru

l) Video

VLC Player - from the Windows DAUM PotPlayer Store - potplayer.ru

SPB TV (view free TV channels on your computer) - from the Windows Store

m) Photo

XnView - xnview.com

Adobe Photoshop Express - From the Store

Windows PhotoFunia - From the Windows Store

PicsArt - From the Windows Store

n) Communication

Skype * - from the Windows Store

Social networks

Facebook * - from the Windows Store
VKontakte * - from the Windows Store

o) E-books

Windows Adobe Reader - From the Windows Store

p) Travel

SkyScanner (search and purchase of airline

tickets) - from the Windows Store

TripAdvisor (Search and Book Hotels) - From the Windows Store

## 2. Screen recording without third-party programs

Users of computers running Windows 10 have the ability to record video from any application or game without the help of third-party programs. To do this, while in a program or game, press the key combination Win + Alt + R.

Video recording will start instantly. Newer versions of Windows 10 have no recording restrictions. In the first builds, recording can be performed only if the program or game is open in full screen. Recorded videos will be stored in the "/ Video / Clips" folder.

## 3. Notifications of ready-to-install updates

Windows is regularly updated, sometimes it seems that almost daily. And the most unpleasant thing infrequent updates is that they begin to be installed automatically and usually at the most inopportune moment. In Windows 10, there is a way to change the operation of the update system, making it less annoying. Windows updates will only download automatically, and the choice of time for installing them will be left to the user.

To do this, you need to run the Run utility (Win + R) and enter the gpedit.msc command in it. In the menu that opens, "Local Group Policy Editor", select the "Administrative Templates" option (in the "Computer Configuration" section) → "Windows Components" → "Windows Update".

Next, in the right column, you need to select the "Configure automatic updates" script and check the "Enabled" box.

## 4. Shake to collapse

One of the most rarely used gestures in Windows 10 is "Shake to minimize." The operating system makes it possible to minimize all open Windows except one really necessary in an extremely original way.

To do this, left-click on the Window title, which must be left open, and shake the Window left and right. As a result of using this non-standard gesture, all open Windows will be minimized, but the only one you select will remain open.

## 5. Protection and security for your peace of mind

The Internet is a dangerous thing, and through public Wi-Fi networks, along with the files you need, something very bad can fly into your computer. Most often, users do not think about the need to install antiviruses until it is too late, so Microsoft took care of their security in advance. In Windows 10, by default, built-in and very effective (if you do not forget to update them) protection tools are installed. Firstly, it is the Windows Defender antivirus program. Secondly, the Windows firewall, which helps to stop the activity of hackers and malware on all wireless networks that the user connects to.

In addition, a special security filter is built into the Microsoft Edge browser. And if children use your computer, then you can use the parental control function: set the intervals for turning on and off the computer, enable or disable specific programs, and, of course, disable access to sites where it would be better for kids not to look at them.

Also, immediately after buying a PC, you must definitely configure the "Search for device" function. If suddenly a disaster strikes and your computer disappears, you can first try to find it by GPS, and if it was not possible, then at least completely block it. And to protect against unauthorized access, there is a Windows Hello feature - hands reaching for other people's personal data will not get anything, and you yourself can unlock the system just by smiling at the webcam.

## 6. Touch input for travel and web surfing

Touch input support in Windows appeared a long time ago, but for some reason, some users still think that there is nothing useful in this. In addition, very in vain! Of course, constantly poking a finger at the screen is really uncomfortable, but there are situations where this can be very appropriate. For example, when you fly on an airplane: you can put a transformer laptop in front of you and enjoy watching a movie. And run it or pause with your fingers. Touch input will help with web surfing and reading e-books in the event that you do not have a mouse with a wheel at hand. Moreover, flipping with your fingers all kinds of online catalogs on the screen is completely a pleasure.

## 7. Details of used and free disk space

In Windows 10, users have the opportunity to get the most detailed information about how much space is taken up on the computer's hard Drive or SSD. Moreover, the new "tens" function tells which files take up space.

To access this information, go to the "Settings" → "System" → "Storage" menu.

## 8. Work with a pen to increase productivity and creativity

Without touch input, it would be impossible to implement another important feature called Windows Ink. Yes, the latest Microsoft operating version supports a digital pen. At first glance, it seems that there is no need to acquire another additional gadget, but this is the story about which they say: "It is worth trying once, and then it will not be easy to live without it."

In addition to the obvious advantage in the form of the ability to leave handwritten notes on different documents and then send them in the form of screenshots for revision to your subordinates or modify them yourself, the pen allows for handwriting input. If, for example, you have a lightweight laptop-transformer, then you can "print" on it even while standing in public transport.

But this is only the beginning. Using the pen is incredibly convenient to bring presentations and text files to the ideal. Need to delete a word? Just cross it out! Need to single out a whole paragraph? Enough to circle him. Plus with a pen, it is easy to move and transform drawings and graphs. And you can quickly write a mathematical formula by hand and then with one click convert it into an object for insertion into the document you need.

You can also use the pen to create complete

drawings right on the screen. A virtual ruler and many additional special tools will help. But in general, everything is limited only by the possibilities of your imagination. Windows Ink is an incredibly powerful tool to make work more convenient and creative.

## 9. File Sharing for Interaction with Colleagues

Along with recent updates in Windows 10, the

"Share with devices" feature has been added. With its help, files from your computer can be very quickly and easily shared with users of nearby devices. Just click on the "Share" button, and then the system itself will find the most optimal way to do this via Wi-Fi or Bluetooth. It is extremely convenient at meetings, for example, or during project work when the task is divided into parts, each of which is performed by a specific employee. Well, it's also useful at home when something needs to be quickly transferred from a laptop to a home PC with a large monitor.

## 10. Block notifications to focus on an important task

You were about to sit down and work hard, but three messages arrived instantly in the messengers, a notification about new emails appeared and the newsletter arrived from your favorite site. It is difficult in such a situation to pull yourself together and finish the ill-fated course, is not it? Windows 10 will help you with the new Focus Attention feature. This is such a special thing that completely blocks all system sounds and incoming notifications. A small sip of digital detox in the harsh modern world of high technology.

At the same time, of course, the user himself sets the interval of the function and can choose a circle of close or simply important people who can always breakthrough with their messages through this reliable shield. Well, after the course is successfully completed, all notifications will immediately appear, and you can carefully study them.

## 11. Code writer

A free text and code editor that supports more than two dozen different syntaxes, which is useful to developers. It has code highlighting, a built-in project manager, a convenient menu of tools and integration with the clouds to save your files.

## 12.   Paint 3D: creating a new image

Before you start working with Paint 3D, make sure that you have this program installed. If you use Windows 10, Paint 3D is built into your system by default. If this is not the case, you can download Paint 3D for free from the Microsoft app store.

Launch Paint 3D and click on the "Create" button to create a new image.

## 13.   Paint 3D Menu

Paint 3D has the main menu, the elements of which you can use to edit the image.

• In the far right corner, you will find graphic tools where you can select various brushes and other tools and draw them.

• Using the "2D" button, you have the opportunity to create two-dimensional shapes, for example, a square.2D-shapes in

## Paint 3D

• On the right is the "3D" button, which you will need if you want to add various 3D models (people, animals, etc.) and figures (sphere, cube, etc.) to your image. You can also create 3D sketches with soft and sharp edges and set various properties of the surface of the object (matte surface, gloss, etc.). 3D models in Paint 3D

• Next to the "3D" button, you can find the "Sticker" button. Stickers can be easily placed on a three-dimensional object. For example, you can create a globe from a sphere and an image with a world map. More on this will be described below.

• Nearby you will find the "Text" button, which you can use to add text to your image.

• The "Effects" button allows you to apply various filters or change the lighting level of your image.

• The "Drawing Area" button is used less often than the others. For example, with it, you can resize the drawing area or select a transparent background.

• Among others, there is also a "Remix 3D" button, where you will find various 3D models that have been downloaded by users. All buttons on the Paint 3D menu

• On the left side of the page, you will find a menu button with which you can save or export your project.


## 14.    How to properly configure Paint 3D

Since Paint 3D mainly creates three-dimensional images, you need to make friends with the special management of this program.

As with the regular Paint editor, you can scale the image using the mouse wheel. And if you click on the button in the upper right corner, you can move and rotate the three-dimensional image using the right mouse button. By clicking on the mouse wheel the image can be moved.

## 15. Paint 3D: creating the first project

In order for you to understand how to work in Paint 3D, we suggest you create the first project with our step by step instructions.

1. First, add a sphere using the 3D button. When creating a sphere, hold the Shift key to make it flat, not ellipsoid.

2. Then download the Earth image from the Internet and drag it into Paint 3D. After that, click on the "Create 3D" button on the right.

3. Now click "Create Sticker".

4. Move the image to the sphere by pressing the left mouse button and scale it so that everything is visible. After that, click on the checkmark. You now have a three-dimensional model of the Earth.

5. Activate the transparent drawing area using the "Symbol Area" button.

6. Export your project by clicking the project management button as an FBX file that you

can open using the Mixed Reality Viewer program. In Windows 10, it is preinstalled.

## A few tricks for a text editor

## 16. Change of register.

It often happens that the user types a piece of text with the Caps Lock key pressed, which turns on the capitalization mode. Many in this case start typing again. However, if you press the key combination Shift + F3 or Shift + F2, then the case of the selected text can be changed automatically.

## 17. Create screenshots.

If you write some kind of instruction and you need to include screenshots (screenshots or Windows) in it, then in addition to the traditional Print Screen key, in Word you can use an internal function called "Snapshot."

Open the "Insert" tab, click on the "Snapshot" button »And in the drop-down menu you will see icons of open Windows. It remains only to choose the necessary.

## 18.   Stress

Sometimes it is necessary to emphasize words. In Word, this is done very simply - place the cursor after the letter on which the stress should be and while holding the Alt key, type the code 769 (this is called the Alt sequence). The numbers need to be dialed on the right, digital, or else they say "gray" keyboard. Please note that in my screenshot in the word "put" the stress is directed in the opposite direction. It is set in the same way, only the code will be 768.

## 19. Password protection.

Word documents can be password protected. Click "File" and select the appropriate function. It is important to remember that if you forget the password, the document cannot be restored.

## 20. Hyphenation.

Hyphenation can help improve document readability. They will not allow the program to make large gaps between words, so that the text will look much neater. Hyphenation can be done manually, but it takes a long time. Automatic insertion can be implemented through the tab "Page Layout" - "Hyphenation".

## 21. Autosave.

Although Word already has AutoSave document enabled, the time interval between saves can be quite large (the default is usually 10 minutes). And precisely because of this interval, most of the text that you have already typed may not be saved. Therefore, it is logical to reduce this time.

Click "File" - "Options" - "Saving" and set the required interval in minutes. I recommend setting the minimum value, that is, "1 minute".

## 22.   One space.

This is not even a tip, but rather a small rule. Never move text with spaces; use Tabs, Word ruler capabilities, footers and so on. Remember - there should always be only one space between words in Word, otherwise when printing, your document will not be ripped at all in the places where you need it.

If it so happened that you had to work with someone else's document, where there are many spaces between words, then you can automatically replace the number of spaces with one. Select the entire text or fragment where replacement is required. On the "Home" tab, in the right part, click the "Replace" button.

In the Window that opens, in the "Find" field, enter two spaces, and in the "Replace with:" field, enter one space, then click the "Replace All" button. If your text contains cases where there are many more gaps, then this procedure must be repeated for each number: 3 on 1; 4 on 1; 5 on 1 and so on.

## 23. One Enter

The same rule applies to the Enter key. Never break text with "enters" to transfer text to a new sheet. To do this, use the "Page Break" function on the "Insert" tab.

Remember: the Enter key breaks the text into paragraphs and automated Word "considers" each "enter" as a full paragraph with typed text, even if it is actually not there. This means that when printing it may well happen that half of the text will be on one sheet, and the other half on the other.

To increase the intervals between texts, headings, etc., use the options from the

"Paragraph" section of the "Home" tab.

## 24. AutoCorrect

This function allows you to assign special indices to words, phrases, and word combinations. If you subsequently detect such an index, Word will immediately replace it with the desired phrase or phrase. For example, in order not to constantly write "Microsoft Word" manually, you can add such an index "MW" and Word will automatically write the entire phrase.

This is done simply. Open the menu "File" - "Options" - "Spelling".

In the Window that opens, the "AutoCorrect Settings" button will be available, by clicking on which all the necessary parameters will become available.

**25.** If you enter notepad.setup in the Run Window, Notepad opens, however, you cannot enter a single word into it, because he will curl up all the time.

**26.** Launch uTorrent, go to Help> About> and click on the icon. You will hear a rather funny sound. And if you press the English "T", you can play the famous Tetris in all of us while your torrent is downloading.

**27.** Open WinRar, go to the Help - About the Program and click on the stack of books. They begin to slowly fall down and then bounce back, and so 10 times.

**28.** "God Mode" - convenient access to system settings

Would you like to become the master of Windows? Then this topic is for you. God Mode allows you to access more than 270 system settings in a convenient order. All you need to do is create a new folder with this name: GodMode. {ED7BA470-8E54-465E-825C-99712043E01C} Then open it and configure the system to your needs.

## 29. Resource monitor

Sometimes it happens that you are working in a program, and it suddenly freezes for no reason and stops responding. The logical action in this situation is to complete the process through the Windows task manager. However, completing the program this way you may lose important data. To avoid this, it is better to act differently. Open the run Window, which we already know, and enter "resmon" in the line. The "Resource Monitor" system tool was launched. In the Window we see all the processes running on the computer. And the process that does not respond will be lit in red. We right-click on it and select "Waiting Chain Analysis". And here we see exactly which process prevents the program from working. If this process is not very important, then you can complete it by returning the operability to our program and keeping all the data intact.

## 30. Mixed reality for new experiences

Any computer with the Windows 10 operating system is a ready-made portal to the world of augmented and virtual reality. The OS is integrated by default with support for the Windows Mixed Reality platform, which means that at any time you can purchase Acer, Dell, HP or Lenovo headset to go to a cozy house on a cliff above the ocean. In this form, Microsoft developers presented an interface in which all your VR and AR programs will be assembled, whether it be games, movies or even software for work.

## 31. Timeline for returning to the past

They say that you can't teleport to the past, but Windows 10 miraculously allows you to do it! To do this, the operating system has a thing called "Timeline". This is the history of all your actions on all devices used, including those based on iOS and Android. It can not only be viewed but also returned with its help to incomplete documents or images and videos. Well, if suddenly it scares you, then the function can simply not be turned on. It is also possible to delete those recorded actions that are no longer relevant to you.

## 32. Dictation and contact organizer for your convenience

Tired of printing long documents? No problem: just start dictating them through the microphone, and Windows 10 will type for you. This is also convenient if you work in a creative industry where every passing thought has a chance to turn into a serious and successful project.

In addition, in a recent update, Windows 10 has learned to work with contacts much better. Ten of the most important can be taken directly to the taskbar, and all the rest can be arranged as you like. In addition, an animation appeared on the People icon.

## 33. Gamepad for your entertainment

Work is work, but you shouldn't forget about rest too. Windows 10 will help you with this, if, of course, computer games are not alien to you. To do this, a special game panel is built into the system from which you can activate the game mode. In it, all additional functions of the operating  system are turned off, and the computing resources freed from this are used to increase gaming performance. Winning is sometimes very tangible.

In addition, using the game panel it is convenient to take screenshots of interesting moments without distracting from the game or record short videos. Plus, right from here you can make broadcasts in Mixer - the new streaming service from Microsoft.

## 34.   Edit Startup List

Everyone knows that at the same time as the Windows shell loads a great many programs and utilities. An antivirus, for example, or a keyboard switch, Skype, etc. Initially, there are relatively few such programs, but after installation, many utilities and software packages silently add themselves to our startup. If the programs are needed, such as the same antivirus - well, we will have to put up with this. But without many programs, you can safely do without. Particularly "lucky" owners of laptops, whose operating system is literally crammed with all kinds of branded gadgets. No, you don't need to delete them, you just need to wean them from the habit of starting independently, at the start of the computer. If we suddenly need them, no one will bother to start these programs manually ...

Now we just have to get to the startup menu - after all,

must the "control panel" exist in the whole zoo? The answer is yes, but only partially.

Windows 10 has an autoload control center - in one of the tabs of the Task Manager - as we recall, it can be launched by right-clicking on the Taskbar at the bottom of the screen and selecting the appropriate link in the context menu. Here you can see a list of programs and modules that start when Windows starts. And not just see, but also turn off unnecessary programs using the same right mouse button.

You can also edit the autorun list using special integrated programs for "tweaking" the system - such as CCleaner, Glary Utilities or AnVir Task Manager: some of these utilities display a much more complete list of autorun programs than the standard Windows customizer.

Which programs should be left at startup, and which ones should be deleted? The question is complex and it is definitely difficult to answer. Personally, I always turn off the startup of modules such as Adobe Reader, Java Update and Google Update - this does not give a noticeable gain in download speed ...

## 35. Disk Cleanup

There are a lot of types of "junk" files, but let's try to name at least their main categories:

• Backup copies of documents and program files - files with the extension bak, old and some others. Almost all files that have the ~ ("tilde") symbol in their extension also belong to the "backup" files. Finally, backed up documents that Microsoft Word creates while running have the wbk extension. Upon completion of the work on the document, they can be deleted, but before that you should not touch such files: they will be needed for automatic recovery of documents in the event of a failure.

• Temporary files. They are created during the operation of any Windows programs and, in principle, should be deleted automatically upon its completion. But it often happens that these files somehow beg the "right to life" from the operating  system and remain in their places of deployment. It's fortunate that there are few such places.

• Error reporting and memory dumps. The latter are capable

• "Gnaw off" several gigabytes from the hard Drive  at once.

• Saved contents of "lost clusters". These files with the Chk extension are created by the doctor program. While checking the hard Drive . As a rule, these files can be found in the "root" folder of the hard Drive . Remove them without fear, because their benefits are zero.

• Temporary files in the browser cache.

They can be attributed to the "garbage" only conditionally - these files are necessary to speed up the loading of frequently visited pages. However, once a month the cache should still be cleared so as not to litter it with "dead" contents.

• Windows Recycle Bin Content. files deleted by you are tracked in the Trash - the system moves them there in case you suddenly need to recover any important document deleted by mistake.

Is it all? Of course, not, the list of "junk" files and recommendations for their removal can be extended to another couple of pages. However, we will do simpler by contacting specialized "cleaner" programs for help, who know better than us what is needed on our disk and what is not. We can only adjust their work. And very carefully monitor them and their actions - otherwise it is not difficult to remove something you need in the cleaning heat ...

Let us start with automation: the new version of Windows 10 can automatically remove some part of the garbage from the disk - say, to clear the Recycle Bin and temporary files.

Go to the Settings □ System □ Storage menu: here you can see how badly your hard Drive  or SSD is clogged and the free space does not end. Actually, this information can also be found in Explorer: the amount of available space is indicated directly below each disk.

But still, the Options □ System □ Storage menu gives us many more options - here you can enable the auto-cleaning system (section Memory control).

For a more complete disk cleaning, you will need a special program. There is such a cleaner (Disk Cleanup program) in any version of Windows: a link to it can be found, for example, on the top button bar of the Explorer in the Control section. Or, which is much easier, through Search by typing the Disk Cleanup command.

Using the Clear System files tab, you free up even more space by sending files from previous Windows installations (they remain on disk after a system update), unnecessary Drive r packages and system logs to oblivion. And by clicking on the Advanced tab in the same section, you can clear unnecessarily

## 36. Recovery Points

Thus, at the first full cleaning, you can free up to several tens of gigabytes of disk space ... This is very useful, especially if you use a fast SSD as a system disk, the volume of which is relatively small. As usual, the standard "cleaner" has many alternatives. Take the free CCleaner program (www.CCleaner.com), which is even more accurate. However, it is much more often used for "covering tracks": CCleaner can clear the history and cache of your browser, search query lists, saved forms and cookies, as well as the history of open documents in various programs. In addition, CCleaner can also delete errors from the registry - maybe not as carefully as other programs, but for free.

Before starting CCleaner for the first time, check the following items in the Windows section:

• Internet Explorer - "Temporary Internet files" and "Index.dat files";

• System - all but the last two;

• Others - all but the last.

For Firefox users, I also recommend that you go to the Applications section and check the boxes in the section:

Firefox - points two and three.

If you want to completely delete information about your adventures on the Internet from your computer, activate the History and List of entered addresses section of Internet Explorer and Firefox.

I recommend that you leave the remaining items blank - at least until you figure out what each of them means.

## 37. Remove programs from Startup

Many users, when starting Windows, automatically download many programs that you don't need to work with, but only increase the startup time and load RAM. So that they themselves do not start, you need to exclude them from startup. To do this, again open the "Run" and enter the command "msconfig". We get into the "System Configuration" Window. By going to the "Startup" tab, you can uncheck the boxes next to those programs that you do not need when starting Windows.

## 38. Automatic bootloader recovery

The Windows 10 recovery environment offers a boot recovery option that works surprisingly well and in most cases is sufficient (but not always). To restore the bootloader in this way, do the following:

95

Boot from a Windows 10 recovery disc or a bootable USB flash Drive  with Windows 10 in the same bit capacity as your system (disk). You can use the Boot Menu to select the Drive to boot.

In the case of booting from the installation Drive , on the screen after selecting the language in the lower left, click System Restore.

Select Troubleshooting, and then select Startup Repair. Select the target operating system. The further process will be performed automatically.

Upon completion, you will either see a message stating that the recovery failed, or the computer will automatically restart (do not forget to return the boot from the hard Drive  to the BIOS) to the restored system (but not always).

If the described method did not help to solve the problem, we turn to a more effective, manual method.

## 39.   Manual recovery procedure

To restore the bootloader, you will need either a Windows 10 distribution kit (bootable USB flash Drive  or disk) or a Windows 10 recovery disk. If you haven't got them, you will have to use another computer to create them. For more information on how to make a recovery disk, see the article Restoring Windows 10.

The next step is to boot from the specified media by placing the boot from it in the BIOS (UEFI), or using the Boot Menu. After loading, if it is an installation flash Drive  or disk, on the language selection screen, press Shift + F10 (the command line will open). If it is a recovery disk, select Diagnostics - Advanced Options - Command Prompt from the menu. At the command prompt, enter three commands in order (after each press Enter):

1. diskpart

2. list volume

3. exit

As a result of the list volume command, you will see a list of connected volumes. Remember the letter of the volume on which the Windows 10 files are located (during the recovery process, this may not be the C partition, but the partition under some other letter).

In most cases (there is only one Windows 10 OS on the computer, a hidden EFI or MBR partition is available), in order to restore the bootloader, it is enough to run one command after that:

bcdboot c: \ Windows (where instead of C you may need to specify a different letter, as mentioned above).

Note: if there are several OSs on the

computer, for example, Windows 10 and 8.1, you can run this command twice, in the first case, specifying the path to the files of one OS, in the second - the other (it will not work for Linux and XP. For 7 depends on configurations).

After executing this command, you will see a message stating that the download files were created successfully. You can try to restart the computer in normal mode (by removing the bootable USB flash Drive  or disk) and check whether the system boots up (after some failures, the download does not take place immediately after the bootloader is restored, but after checking the HDD or SSD and rebooting, the error 0xc0000001 may also appear, which is the case is also usually fixed by a simple reboot).

# Conclusion

According to the latest data published by NetMarketShare, Windows 10 is finally considered the most popular desktop operating system.

Its share is currently 39.22%, although it is still inferior to Windows 7. The latter today owns 36.9%. Over time, the backlog of

Windows 7 will only increase.

Windows 10 turned out to be a more complete and well-thought-out system compared to Windows 8 - both corny in terms of appearance and in terms of the concept itself. Instead of trying to make a layer cake from two completely alien systems, Microsoft proposed a single system and universal applications for it, which should look the same wherever they run - on a desktop, tablet or smartphone. As a result, now in Windows 10, it is not always possible to say with certainty which application in front of you is a modern universal, "old" Metro or even a classic desktop one.

do not, of course, forget that Microsoft plans to actively support Windows 10 with the constant release of updates - moreover, according to her, this is the last Windows that is released according to the old scheme, and then it turns into "Windows as a service" - without major releases, revision of the concept, etc., but with regular updates, thanks to which Microsoft (and the developers of Windows applications) will be sure that all users currently have the most current version of the system installed. It's hard to say what actually comes of this, and whether Windows 10 will really be Microsoft's latest OS - but if so, then this is a good enough system to dwell on.

**I hope, that you really enjoyed reading my book.**

**Thanks for buying the book anyway!**

Made in the USA
Middletown, DE
27 January 2020